■SCHOLASTIC
News
Nonfiction Readers

Math in the Backyard

by Ellen Weiss

Children's Press®
A Division of Scholastic Inc.
New York Toronto London Auckland Sydney
Mexico City New Delhi Hong Kong
Danbury, Connecticut

These content vocabulary word builders are for grades 1–2.

Math Consultant: Linda K. Voges, EdD, Cohort Coordinator/Lecturer,
College of Education, The University of Texas at Austin

Reading Consultant: Cecilia Minden-Cupp, PhD, Early Literacy Consultant and Author,
Chapel Hill, North Carolina

Photographs © 2008: Corbis Images/Craig Tuttle: 5 bottom left, 12; iStockphoto/Digitalvisions: 2, 4 bottom right, 15; James Levin Studios: 19; JupiterImages/Kindra Clineff/Index Stock Imagery: 9; Peter Arnold Inc./Jean-Michel Labat/PHONE: 21; PhotoEdit: 17 (Michael Newman), back cover, 7 (Frank Siteman); The Image Works/Bob Daemmrich: cover; VEER/E. J. Carr/Solus Photography: 1, 13.

Book Design: Simonsays Design!
Book Production: The Design Lab

Library of Congress Cataloging-in-Publication Data
Weiss, Ellen, 1949–
Math in the backyard / by Ellen Weiss.
    p. cm. — (Scholastic news nonfiction readers)
Includes bibliographical references and index.
ISBN-13: 978-0-531-18529-2 (lib. bdg.) 978-0-531-18782-1 (pbk.)
ISBN-10: 0-531-18529-X (lib. bdg.) 0-531-18782-9 (pbk.)
1. Mathematics—Juvenile literature. I. Title. II. Series.
QA40.5.W4448 2008
510-dc22   2007005864

CONTENTS

WORD HUNT

Look for these words as you read. They will be in **bold**.

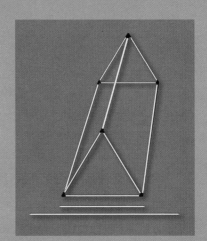

diagram
(**dye**-uh-gram)

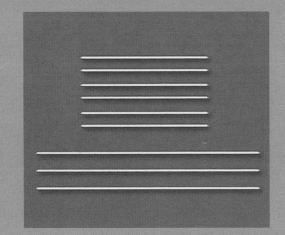

poles
(pohlz)

sunrise
(**sun**-rize)

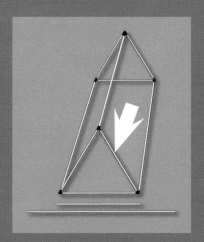

line
(line)

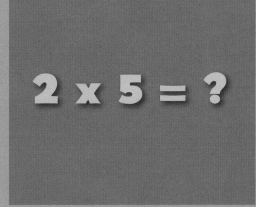

multiplication
(muhl-tuh-pluh-**kay**-shun)

sunset
(**sun**-set)

Sunrise	Sunset
5:44 A.M.	8:22 P.M.

table
(**tay**-buhl)

A Yard of Math

Let's go outside!

We can have lots of fun in our backyard.

Let's see how many ways we can use math.

We use math when we play hopscotch.

We're going to sleep in our tent tonight!

First, we need to put our tent together.

We'll work together
to put up the tent.

We have a **diagram**.
It shows how the tent **poles** fit together.

There are two sizes of poles, short and long.

Look at the white arrow on the next page.

It points to a **line**.

Does that line show a short pole or a long pole?

Turn to page 23 for the answer.

Diagram

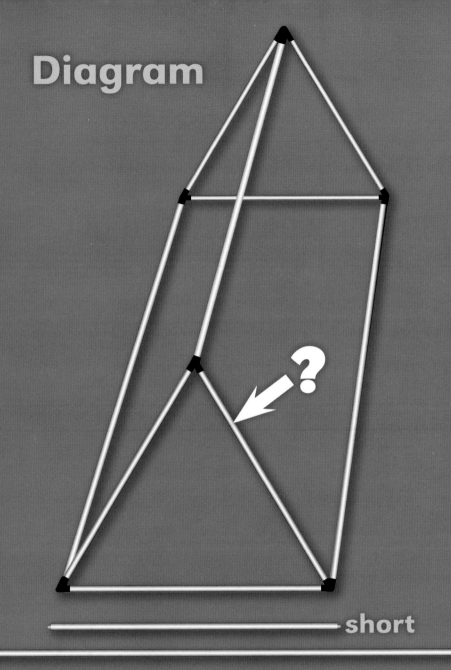

short

long

poles

11

We will go to sleep after **sunset**.

Sunset is when the sun goes down and it starts to get dark.

Sunrise is when the sun comes up in the morning.

The sun will wake us up!

sunset

It gets dark outside soon
after the sun sets.

We want to know what time the sun will wake us up.

We look at a **table** to see when sunrise and sunset will be.

Do you think we'll sleep past 6 o'clock in the morning?

Turn to page 23 for the answer.

Sunrise	Sunset
5:44 A.M.	8:22 P.M.

table

15

We woke up early! Today, we will plant the garden.

We're going to plant pumpkins.

We're making holes in the ground for the seeds.

We need to dig
one hole for
every plant we
want to grow.

We need to dig a hole for each of our seeds.

We have 2 packets of seeds.

Each packet has 5 seeds.

How many holes do we need?

You can use **multiplication** or addition to find the answer.

Turn to page 23 for the answer.

2 x 5 = ? or 5 + 5 = ?

VEGETABLES   Net Wt. 4.2 gm

HOWDEN
PUMPKIN
5 Seeds

VEGETABLES   Net Wt. 4.2 gm

HOWDEN
PUMPKIN
5 Seeds

At last, our planting is done.

Now the worms are working.

Worms are good for the soil.

Look at the worms in the picture.

I wonder how many worms are in the whole garden!

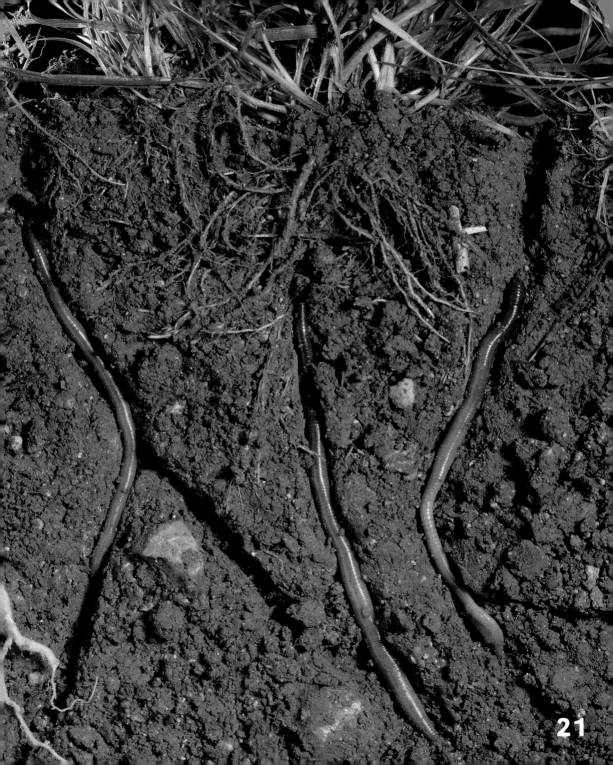

YOUR NEW WORDS

diagram (**dye**-uh-gram) a drawing or plan that shows the parts of something or explains something

line (line) a set of points that forms a straight path

multiplication (muhl-tuh-pluh-**kay**-shun) the process of adding the same number to itself several times

poles (pohlz) long, smooth pieces of metal, plastic, wood, or other material

sunrise (**sun**-rize) the time in the morning when the sun appears above the horizon

sunset (**sun**-set) the time in the evening when the sun disappears below the horizon

table (**tay**-buhl) a chart that lists facts or figures

ANSWERS

Page 10

The white arrow is pointing to a short line, so you need to choose a short pole to fit that line.

Page 14

The table on page 15 shows that the sun will rise at 5:44 A.M. You will probably be awake by 6:00 A.M. because it will be light by then.

Page 18

There are 2 packets. Each packet contains 5 seeds.
2 x 5 = 10
You could also use the number sentence **5 + 5 = 10**. You need to dig **10** holes.

INDEX

FIND OUT MORE

Book:

Weiskopf, Catherine, Marilyn Burns, and Cristina Ong (illustrator). *Lemon & Ice & Everything Nice.* New York: Scholastic, 2002.

Website:

PrimaryGames: Four Piece Tangram
www.primarygames.com/math/tangram/start.htm

MEET THE AUTHOR

Ellen Weiss has received many awards for her books for kids. She lived in England for a short time, where people say "maths" instead of "math."